The Nature Kid's Guide to
BEES

DAVID ANDERSON

LP Media Inc. Publishing
Text copyright © 2026 by LP Media Inc.
All rights reserved.

For information address LP Media Inc. Publishing,
30012 Variolite St NW, Princeton MN 55371
www.lpmedia.org

Publication Data

Bees
The Nature Kid's Guide to Bees — First edition.

Summary: "Learn all about Bees, the Nature Kid Way"
— Provided by publisher.

ISBN: 979-8-89818-198-7

[1. Bees – Non-Fiction] I. Title.

Title: The Nature Kid's Guide to Bees

CONTENTS

BUZZING BEYOND

Bees can recognize human faces — scientists tested this and found they can tell people apart just like we can!

Buzzz! A bumblebee zips past a field of bright flowers.

Bees are some of the busiest creatures on Earth. They live in gardens, forests, hot deserts, and almost everywhere in between.

There are more than 20,000 kinds of bees! That means there are more bee species than all the birds and mammals combined! Some bees are as small as a grain of rice. Others, like bumblebees, are pretty big!

Not all bees look the same either. Many have yellow and black stripes. Others shine bright blue or green like tiny flying jewels. Every single kind of bee is special in its own way.

BUZZING BODIES

A bee's tongue works like a straw to sip sweet nectar. It can be longer than the bee's whole head!

Whirr! Tiny wings beat so fast they become a blur.

A bee's body has three main parts: a head, a thorax, and an abdomen. Each part has an important job to do.

The head alone is packed with tools. Two large compound eyes sit on the sides, and three tiny eyes rest on top. That gives bees five eyes total! Six legs help them walk, grip flowers, and carry pollen back to the nest.

Two pairs of clear wings let bees fly fast and far. They beat 200 times per second — that buzzing sound you hear is those wings working hard. Tiny hairs covering the entire body act like velcro, grabbing pollen from every flower a bee visits.

WAGGLE WONDERS

A honeybee hive keeps itself at about 95 degrees inside — even on freezing winter days!

Tap, tap, tap! Bees build tiny wax rooms inside the hive.

Honeybees live together in a **hive**. A single hive can hold up to 60,000 bees! The queen bee lays eggs. Worker bees build, clean, and guard the hive.

Workers make wax from their bodies. They shape it into tiny six-sided rooms called cells. Baby bees grow inside some cells. Other cells store food for the **colony**.

When a bee finds flowers, it does a waggle dance. It moves in a special pattern to tell other bees where to go. The dance is like a map that shows direction and distance!

POLLEN PIONEERS

One honeybee can visit up to 5,000 flowers in a single day — that's more than three flowers every minute!

Poof! A cloud of golden pollen covers the bee's fuzzy body.

Flowers need **pollen** to make seeds. Bees carry pollen from one flower to the next. This is called pollination. Without it, new plants could not grow.

When a bee lands on a flower, pollen sticks to its fuzzy body. The bee flies to another flower and some pollen falls off. That flower can now make fruit or seeds.

One out of every three bites of food we eat starts with a bee visit. Bees help grow apples, berries, almonds, and many other foods we love.

12

Thrumm! Thousands of honeybees swarm around their queen.

Honeybees are the most famous bees in the world. They live in big groups called colonies. Each colony has one queen, many workers, and some **drones**. Every bee has a job.

Worker bees gather nectar and pollen. Drones help the queen. When a colony gets too crowded, the queen leaves with half the bees to find a new home. This is called a swarm!

A single colony can make over 60 pounds of honey a year!

Honeybees must visit about two million flowers to make just one pound of honey!

BUZZING BUMBLEBEES

A queen bumblebee sleeps underground all winter, then wakes up in spring to start a brand new nest!

Brrr! A fat bumblebee flies out on a chilly spring morning.

Bumblebees are round, fuzzy, and built for the cold. Their thick fur traps warmth so well that they can fly on chilly days when other bees stay home.

Bumblebees nest underground, often moving into an abandoned mouse hole. Their colonies are cozy and small, with just 50 to 400 bees compared to the tens of thousands in a honeybee hive.

These bees have a superpower called buzz pollination. They grab onto a flower and vibrate their bodies at just the right speed to shake the pollen loose. Tomatoes, peppers, and blueberries all depend on this special technique to grow their best fruit.

DRILLING DWELLINGS

Crunch! A carpenter bee chews a round hole into a log.

Carpenter bees make their homes in wood. They chew round tunnels into dead trees, fence posts, and old sheds. The holes look like someone drilled them with a power tool!

Each tunnel has small rooms inside. The mother bee fills each room with pollen and lays one egg. Then she seals it shut with chewed wood.

Carpenter bees live alone, not in groups. They may look like bumblebees, but their belly is smooth and shiny instead of fuzzy. That is the easiest way to tell them apart.

Most mason bees finish all their nesting work in just four to six weeks, then rest until the next spring.

Plop! A mason bee packs a ball of mud into a tiny hole.

Mason bees are gentle and rarely sting. They live alone and nest in small holes in wood, walls, or hollow stems. These bees are found in many parts of the world.

A mother mason bee gathers mud to build walls inside her nest. She makes a row of tiny rooms. Each room gets pollen, nectar, and one egg.

Mason bees are amazing at spreading pollen. One mason bee can do the work of 100 honeybees! That is why farmers love having them near their crops.

LEAF CUTTERS

Snip! A leafcutter bee slices a neat circle from a green leaf.

Leafcutter bees use their strong jaws like scissors. They cut perfect round circles from leaves and carry each piece back to their nest.

Inside a hollow stem or hole, the bee wraps the leaf pieces into tiny tubes. She places pollen and one egg inside each tube. The soft leaf keeps the baby safe and snug.

Leafcutter bees are solitary, which means they live alone. You can spot their work by looking for leaves with neat, round holes cut from the edges.

KILLER BEES

FUN FACT!

Killer bees make just as much honey
as regular honeybees — they are
simply more protective of their hive!

Zzzzz! A swarm of killer bees bursts from a crack in a wall.

Killer bees got their start in a science lab. In 1956, people crossed African bees with local bees in Brazil. Some escaped and spread to new places.

Killer bees look just like honeybees. You cannot tell them apart by sight! But killer bees get angry faster and chase threats much farther than regular honeybees do.

If you see a swarm, stay calm and walk away slowly. Killer bees only sting when they feel their home is in danger. On their own, they are just busy bees doing their job.

FLYING JEWELS

There are over 200 kinds of orchid bees, and each species shines a different dazzling color!

Whizz! A bright green orchid bee darts through the jungle air.

Orchid bees live in warm, wet jungles in Central and South America. Their bodies glow with bright colors like green, blue, and gold. They look like flying jewels!

Male orchid bees visit orchid flowers to collect sweet smells. They store the smells in special pouches on their back legs. Then they use the scents to attract a mate.

These bees visit many kinds of flowers deep in the jungle. Some orchids can only be pollinated by orchid bees. Without these shiny flyers, those flowers would disappear.

STINGLESS SURVIVORS

There are over 500 kinds of stingless bees, and scientists are still discovering new ones hiding in tropical forests every year!

Hummm! A stingless bee squeezes out of a tiny wax tube.

Stingless bees do have stingers, but they are too small to hurt. These bees live in warm places all year round. Most are found in South America, Africa, and Asia.

Stingless bees build nests inside hollow trees. They use wax and sticky tree sap to hold everything together. A tiny tube acts as the front door to keep enemies out.

So how do they defend themselves? These bees bite! Some even spit a sticky goo at enemies. They make honey too, but their honey tastes more sour than sweet compared to the kind you buy at the store.

MINING MARVELS

Scritch! A mining bee digs a tunnel straight down into dirt.

Mining bees live underground! They dig tunnels in bare soil, sandy paths, and garden lawns. Each mother bee digs her own nest all by herself.

Inside the tunnel, she makes small rooms. She fills each one with pollen and nectar. Then she lays an egg and seals the room with packed dirt.

Mining bees come out in early spring. They are gentle and rarely sting people. If you see small dirt mounds on the ground with tiny holes, a mining bee family may live there.

GLITTERING GUESTS

There are over 3,000 different kinds of sweat bees — some are smaller than a grain of rice!

Zip! A tiny green sweat bee lands on a sweaty arm.

Sweat bees got their name because they like the salt in sweat! They may land on your skin to take a tiny lick. Do not worry. They are very gentle and rarely sting.

These bees are small and shiny. Many glow bright green or blue. They look like bits of flying metal! Some live in tiny holes in the ground. Others nest in old wood.

A few species can even fly at night, which almost no other bee can do. The same species might live alone in spring but form a small colony by summer. Scientists still do not fully understand why!

FUZZY
FLYERS
DID YOU KNOW?
Teddy bear bees only live for
about six to eight weeks as adults!

Brumm! A plump, fuzzy teddy bear bee tumbles into a flower.

Teddy bear bees are named for their thick, golden fur. They look soft and cuddly, just like a toy bear! These bees live only in parts of Australia.

Teddy bear bees dig burrows in clay or soft dirt. Each mother makes her own nest alone. She stocks it with pollen and nectar for her babies to eat when they hatch.

These bees are fast and loud flyers. They buzz from flower to flower and are great at spreading pollen. People in Australia love to see them visit their backyard gardens.

GIANT'S RETURN

Whoosh! The world's biggest bee spreads its giant dark wings.

Wallace's giant bee is the biggest bee on Earth. It can be as big as your thumb! This rare bee lives on just a few small islands in Indonesia.

For many years, no one could find this bee. Scientists thought it might be extinct. Then in 2019, researchers spotted one alive in the wild! It was big news around the world.

This giant bee makes its nest inside termite mounds in trees. It uses sticky tree resin to line and protect the walls. Saving its forest home is the best way to help this amazing bee survive.

BACKYARD BEEKEEPERS

Crack! A beekeeper lifts the lid and peeks inside the hive.

People have kept bees for thousands of years. Beekeepers raise honeybees in special wooden boxes called hives. They collect honey, wax, and pollen to use or sell.

Beekeepers wear white suits and face covers to stay safe. Smoke from a small tool helps keep bees calm during visits. It is a careful, gentle job that takes lots of practice.

Bees help farmers grow food all over the world. Without bees, we would lose many fruits and vegetables. Keeping bees healthy matters for all of us.

BEE BELIEVERS

Zoom! A bee lands in a garden planted by kids just like you.

Bees need our help. Many bees are losing their homes. Buildings, farms, and bug sprays can harm them. Some kinds of bees are now very hard to find.

You can help bees! Plant flowers that bloom at different times of year. Skip the bug spray near gardens. Leave patches of bare dirt for bees that nest in the ground.

Every single bee matters. When you see a bee buzz by, say thank you. That little bee is working hard to keep our world green and growing.

GLOSSARY

colony
A big group of bees that live and work together

drone
A male bee in a colony

hive
A home where a colony of bees lives together

nectar
A sweet liquid inside flowers that bees drink

pollen
A fine yellow powder in flowers that helps plants grow

www.ingramcontent.com/pod-product-compliance
Lightning Source LLC
Chambersburg PA
CBHW041609110726
48005CB00002B/347